FEAR NOT the night that prowls,
for our feet will lead the way.

FEAR NOT
the night
that chatters...

... for our hearts will carry us through.

DO NOT be afraid ...

... of wandering into the night.

DO NOT be afraid...

... of danger lurking.

DO NOT be afraid...

... of **MONSTERS** gathering.

DO NOT be afraid...

... of losing your way.

FEAR NOT the prowling night ...

... our feet will lead the way ...

... and our hearts will carry us through.

DO NOT be afraid,
my little one,

for I am always
beside you.

The night has fallen, and home is here.

When you close your eyes …

... dreams are calling.

Trang Hoang works for Room to Read Vietnam as a writer and editor with a focus on children's picture books. She is passionate about working with children and strongly committed to nurturing their dreams through the power of storytelling.

Pham Quang Phuc works for Kim Dong Publishing House as an art editor and illustrator. Writing for children is a childhood dream come true and he now considers storytelling as a way to balance his life, and hopes young readers will gain interests and dreams from his stories.

As close friends, neighbors and teammates for years, the two of them have worked on several creative projects for children and together won the ASEAN Children's Book Illustrator - Best in Fiction Award at The International Children's Content Rights Fair with their latest project 'Everywhere Monster'.